Puffer Fish

KIDS EXPLORE!

Thanks for checking out the Kids Explore!Series. Please note:All Rights Reserved. No part of this publication may be reproduced in any form or by any means, including scanning, photocopying, or otherwise without prior written permission of the copyright holder. Copyright © 2014

Pufferfish

The Pufferfish is very unique fish. It is also known as the blowfish, globefish, toadfish and balloonfish; we will discover why later on in this book. There are more than 120 species of Pufferfish worldwide. They range from very small to very large. Read on to discover more cool facts about this exciting fish. In this book we will discover all sorts of new and interesting things. So sit back and be prepared to be wowed. Read on….

Where in the World?

Did you know some Pufferfish can live in freshwater? Most Pufferfish live in the warm tropical waters of the ocean. Others can be found in partly salted water or "brackish." Most Puffers can be found around Southeast Asia. One species lives in Central America. Three other species live in the waters off of Central Africa.

The Body of a Pufferfish

Did you know some Pufferfish can get very large? Puffers can measure all the way up to 3 feet long (1 meter). They have long tapered bodies, with a big bulbous head. Some can be very brightly colored. This lets other fish know it is poisonous. The Puffer fish has two eyes high up on its head.

The Pufferfish Has a Special Ability

Did you know the Pufferfish can blow (or puff) itself up? The Pufferfish starts out thin, but when it is scared, it blows itself up. The Puffer does this by taking in huge amounts of water. This turns the Puffer into a big ball and a mean fighting machine. Some even have spikes. This fish is also very poisonous.

The Puffer's Other Abilities

Did you know the Puffer fish swims very slowly? The Puffer uses all its fins to swim through the water. Although it may be slow, it can move in all directions. It uses its tail fin like a rudder on a boat. When the Puffer is frightened, it can burst forward to try and avoid getting caught. Some Puffers also blend in with the bottom of the ocean to stay safe.

The Pufferfish Teeth

Did you know the Pufferfish has teeth? Unlike most fish, the Puffer has very sharp teeth. It has 4 large teeth inside its mouth - 2 on top and 2 on the bottom. These teeth are all joined together. This looks like a beak. The Puffer uses its beak-like teeth to crush its prey. Its teeth are also sharp enough to cut a human finger.

What a Puffer Fish Eats

Did you know the Pufferfish is a carnivore? This means the Puffer prefers to eat meat. This type of fish will eat algae once in a while. Its main diet is invertebrates. Large Pufferfish use their sharp beak-like teeth to crack open clams, mussels and shellfish. Puffers search the ocean floor with their excellent eyesight for a tasty treat.

Enemies of the Pufferfish

Did you know the Puffer is hunted? Even though this fish is toxic, some animals still hunt it. Sharks are the only species that are immune to the Puffer's poison. If a bigger fish gobbles up the Puffer before it inflates, it is still very yucky to taste. People hunt the Pufferfish, as well. Read on to discover how.

Pufferfish and People

Did you know there's enough poison in one Pufferfish to kill 30 humans? Yet humans still hunt the Puffer for its meat. In Japan the Puffer meat is called "Fugu." It is considered a delicacy. Specially trained chef's will cut the Puffer up, so no poison is left. If this fish is not cut up just right, it is still poisonous to eat.

Pufferfish Mom and Dad

Did you know the Pufferfish do not have babies until they are 5 years-old? The dad Puffer fish will guide the female Puffer to shallow water. This is usually near the shore. Once here the mom Puffer will release about 3 to 7 eggs. The male fertilizes the eggs, then they leave and the eggs are left on their own to survive.

Baby Pufferfish

Did you know some Puffer fish young are so small, you can only see them through a magnifying glass? Baby Pufferfish look exactly like the adults. The eggs of the Pufferfish babies are very hard. Once the shells crack open, the young Pufferfish swim towards the rest of the community.

Life of a Pufferfish

Did you know most Puffers can live to be 10 years-old? Some Pufferfish are dropping in their numbers. This is due to hunting, habitat loss and pollution in the water. Some people try to keep Pufferfish as pets. This is very difficult to do. The aquarium must be perfect for a Puffer to live happily.

The Pea Pufferfish

Did you know the Pea Puffer Fish is the smallest one? The Pea Puffer or Dwarf Puffer lives in freshwater. It can be found around Southeast India. It measures less than 1 inch long (22 millimeters). It is yellow with black or dark green patches on its body.

The Giant Pufferfish

Did you know the Giant Puffer lives in the Congo river of Africa? This Puffer can grow to be 26 inches long (67 centimeters). It eats smaller fish, crustaceans and mollusks. It is also called the, Mbu Puffer fish, The skin of this Puffer fish is yellow on the bottom with black and white markings on its body.

Porcupine Fish

Did you know the Porcupine Fish has spikes on it? This fish is a slow swimmer, but it does not matter. When this Puffer fish gets frightened, it blows itself up into a huge ball. But that's not all, it has sharp spikes that poke out all around it. Plus, it is poisonous to eat. That's one prickly snack!

Quiz

Question 1: Some Puffer fish are found in brackish water. What does that mean?

Answer 1: It is partly salted

Question 2: How big can some Puffer's get?

Answer 2: Up to 3 feet long (1 meter)

Question 3: What is the Puffer's special ability?

Answer 3: It can take in water to inflate itself like a big round ball

Question 4: What is the smallest Puffer fish?

Answer 4: The Pea Puffer

Question 5: Which Puffer has spikes on it?

Answer 5: The Porcupine Puffer

Thank you for checking out another title from Kids Explore! Make sure to check out Amazon.com for many other great books.

Made in the USA
Middletown, DE
23 April 2017